THE LAST CUT

By F.M Kay

Published by Accent Press Ltd – 2005
www.accentpress.co.uk

ISBN 0954867378

Printed and bound in Singapore
by Craft Print International .

Cover illustration, *St. Ives Couple II,*
by Trevor Price
www.trevorprice.co.uk

To Sara, with love and hopes for
a lifelong friendship.

And thank you, Anna.

ACKNOWLEDGMENTS

'Missing the Train', 'out of office hours', 'unacceptable behaviour' and 'manicure' have appeared in *Obsessed with Pipework* Magazine.

'balance of power' has appeared in *iota* magazine.

'rain on the windscreen' and 'I think this might be it' have appeared in *Fire* magazine.

'hold onto me' has appeared in *The Ugly Tree* magazine.

'at the theatre' has appeared in *Pulsar* magazine.

Comfortable Silence II
By Trevor Price

INDEX

curves in the passing of time

every time you walk down the hall
and pause by your front door,

      there,
if you want to see it,

is the image of us,
kissing,

my hands on your shoulders,
yours, beneath my clothes, on my waist,

our shared breath warm,
excited,
intense,

the time stolen
from family lives,
from the ordinary goodbyes,

delaying the end of the day.

if you want to see it,
we're still there.

**perhaps it was meant to
be just a social visit**

it nearly didn't happen

but I
yes I think it was me

well I put my hand on
your shoulder

    and stepped towards you
    and I think it was me that

first touched your lips with mine
and that began it

beginnings

a kiss
two kisses

made me shake,

heat circling my hips,
my spine warm,

I pressed against you,
feeling you,
tasting you,

letting everything go
except that moment.

crossing a boundary

there was a slight hesitation
and then we embraced
like we often do on meeting or parting

and in that moment
a barrier disappeared
and we kissed like lovers,

his hands round my waist
and mine on his face,

there was a pause,

then I began to talk, distracted, odd
 thoughts, random phrases, as
 if the world could be put right
put back
somehow somehow
with my words,

but he said nothing,
and then when I fell silent
we kissed again.

afraid

it was only a week ago
that we saw each other naked,
touched each other,
felt the rightness and ease of it.

and now I'm sitting shivering in the car,
so afraid
that it was the only time,
that it won't happen again.

I'm sitting at a red traffic light,
with tears in my eyes
at that almost unbearable thought,
and I have no idea what to do.

only the second time

I looked down the length of my body,
seeing your head
between my legs and
feeling your tongue and fingers and

just before I stopped thinking at all

don't worry no-one can
see us here

the window showed
rainwashed grey and
the street was out of sight
  so far below
but we pulled the curtain
across anyway
in case anyone flew past
on prying neighbour's wings
  and caught sight of us
  doing something in the
  spare bedroom that was
  definitely worth
    whispering about

less than a week ago

I remember how it was to
  touch you and
  taste you
and feel your warmth,

my body can recall it,
my mind has not let it go,

I'm sure I could
bring you here
    just by
closing my eyes,
  thinking very hard,

and wishing it.

lovesick

yes it is an illness,
my whole body is affected,

there are no obvious signs,
I would expect a spreading blush staining
 my skin,
or a bruise perhaps
yes a bruise

and how on earth am I still
walking about,
smiling and talking and laughing
without any symptoms showing at all?

yes I am ill with it
I really am,

and I have only myself to share it with,
no-one else knows, no they don't
and I don't think you do
really
not how ill I actually am

so it's just me
yes me

lovesick

afternoon

I licked my fingers,
drew them across my stomach,
then licked them again,

and sure enough
there was the taste of you
from when we had laid together,

our breath, our sweat,
  everything,
pressed so close,

And that taste,
when I was clothed and
 miles away from you,

brought me the clearest image,
as if we had

returned somehow
 to this morning,
and laid together again.

usually I'm the assertive one

no-one ever before
grabbed my hair
and pulled my head
        forward for
  a brief
        hard kiss

    I liked that feeling of
            not being in control

manicure

for the first time ever

I've started really looking after
my fingernails,

shaping, polishing,
protecting, moisturising,
painting,

spending time and effort,
taking a lot of care,

and I'm doing it because

I want to take you
in my hand,

enfold you, arouse you,

and then remember the image of

my fingers wrapped around you
with their startlingly coloured nails,

when you're so
pale,
beautiful,
erect.

watching

you lay back,

I knelt next to you,

  and I said
Show me how you do it - alone,

then
I watched your hand move,
your body start to tense,
your expression turning inwards,
  away from me,

and I didn't touch you although
I wanted to,

instead,
both doing it alone,
we shared the separate journeys,

and
we came together.

daydreams

I've discovered my
mind really does wander,
  and I feel a little sleepy,

do you know
I can
    picture your beautiful smooth body,
conjure your touch,
feel your grainy soft voice,
celebrate our shared warmth,
hope it's not over between us,
take the long view,

oh
and at the same time
carry on as usual,

with a shimmer of desire
just slightly
altering the now.

finding a way

our hands touched,
and stayed in contact
    as we held the map
    and you pointed out a route.

I was so aware of
the warmth of your skin,

    wondering,
      as I always wonder,
if this contact was accidental,

   thinking,
    as I always think,
that it wasn't,

   and feeling,
    as I always feel,
     both
inhibition and
    desire.

In a way that was the best part

afterwards,
    just before we got up
    and put on our clothes,

  as you lay on the bed

  I moved across you and
    rested my head on your chest
    just below your right shoulder.

Immediately you
    put your arms round me and
    held me very tightly,

and I began to breathe more easily,
and I began to stop shaking,
and I began to grow aware of the room
    and us in it,

  and slowly,
  safe as you held me,

I found my way
back to the everyday world.

time and place

as the lunch hour chat about diets
TV shows
teenage children
and soft furnishings
drifts calmly and contentedly
across the staffroom,

and cellophane food wrappings crackle,
and cutlery scrapes on china plates,

I am a largely unregarded visitor,
sitting quietly in a corner
with my notebook,

and I'm writing about you,
unclothed,
the last time we were together,

and I'm picturing your
beautiful naked body,

and I'm remembering
how you sat across me,
leaning back a little
with fingers
inside me

while I stroked you
and watched your face change
as you came.

I expect some of the teachers
in this staffroom
are wondering why I'm smiling.

holding hands

it is the most intimate thing,
   palm pressed to palm,
    with fingers curving
    round the other's hand.

it seems to mean more than
all other intimacies,

appearing to link
bodies, emotions, spirits,

and if our hands join like this
when we are naked together
and making love,

   there's a moment,
   as our palms meet,

   that makes a
shockingly direct connection.

pictures

if I look up,
our eyes meet,
 I realize
you are watching me
  kneeling next to you,
  my mouth holding you,
  lips caressing you,
  tongue stroking you,

and I briefly wonder
  what picture you see

  as you stretch out your hand
  and gently touch my hair.

the first time we've

as it begins,
your face is so beautiful,
  lost in emotion and
  physical sensation,

we are utterly together
as we
as

then

we are complete
for this moment, and
  I know
there can never be better than this.

some things I'd like to do

I'd like to
dance with you,
dine with you,

   shop with you,

argue a bit,
laugh a lot more,

But most of all
I'd like to wake up with you.

first time since I thought it had ended

I kissed down
the curve of the side of your body,

  and rubbed my cheek across your
  belly with its soft hair,

and I whispered
oh
what was it?

it was something like

'I was so sad when
    I thought I'd never see you
           naked again'

not daring now to look up
    as the words came out
  because
        I didn't want you
          to see my sudden tears.

over reacting

I couldn't help it -
I cried a lot
drove in the very appropriate rain
felt desolate
failed to sleep

walked around feeling
how thin my skin was,
knew I'd lost you forever,

realised your regard had
turned to dislike,
cut myself to make the pain less,

and then
and then
when you phoned,

oh then
of course

you'd been ill
then busy
had your phone switched off,

hadn't really considered me,
and then

I wasn't sure whether or not to let
some anger
drip into

the great flood of my relief.

going into freefall

very early this morning,
  making love
in the usual bed and
in the usual comfortable and
familiar way,

like always,
yes always,

practised and until now mutual
        and entirely happy,

I was thankful
 for the closed curtains and
 the half dark,

as I could not lose
    the image of you from my mind,
    the memory of your touch on my skin,
     the desire for you that never quite leaves me,

and I could not stop my tears.

doing a little magic

a visitor,
left to shower and dress
after
everyone had gone to
start their days,

outside, the spring sun
    shone through cracks in
    drawn curtains,

the house was quiet,
undisturbed by me,
all alone in the space.

I went upstairs
to your bedroom and
walked around it,
around the bed,

then I leant down,
    kissed your pillow, and
    the place where
    you lie every night,

and hoped to leave
something of myself there
    for your dreams.

out of normal office hours

behind the door

no time for subtlety
our kisses
  hard

bodies straining
together

warmth
through clothes

wanting to remove all
but no time
    no time

my half undone jeans
your fingers search and rub

I wriggle away
don't go further

gasping
  for breath

I want you
   stop
someone could come in,

you take away your hand
and
lick your fingers

stepping through the door

up on adrenalin
and a sudden rush of desire,
I'm halfway there already
before your fingers begin,

so standing as we are
    fully clothed and
one door away from the world

my senses heighten,
the tension breaks,
I shudder,
I can barely stand,
only just recognising where I am,

leaning against you,
feeling my heart and
my centre singing out,

but through the red confusion
knowing I must
    find myself again,
enough at least to step outside and
wish everyone good night.

preparation

I gasp and shudder,

the floor no longer
seems flat or level,

it is so so hot,

my vision is completely
blurred,

some part of me
remembers not to cry out,

I'm caught between your body and the wall,

your hand is the only fixed point
in the utter chaos,

I am shaking,
I try to get a grip,

The meeting starts in ten minutes.

unacceptable behaviour

is he in the shower?
yes
    then come here,

I step into the room, it's
warm
dangerous
and so wrong,

but I lean over the bed to kiss you,

you stretch up and stroke my breast
and I
reach under the duvet to caress you,

I can hardly breathe,

you gesture,
insistent between kisses,

lie down
come here
    I can't
     you can

but there's a sound from outside and

I stand,
  excited,
    tingling,
      wet, and

  walk away

I wonder where you are tonight

I want you deep inside

my hips moving with your rhythm

my spine dissolving in warmth

my body sweating beneath you

I want to cry out with the joyful pain of it

And feel you shudder as you come

standing up kissing

I like your height,
turning my face up to yours,

we've already said goodbye
but
    our last kiss has lengthened,

    delaying the moment
when I have to leave,
 and
 your hands start to loosen
 my clothing so recently
put back on as we kiss
 and time slows down,

you're so wet

I always am
 when
I'm with you

whenever I undress

I take pleasure in
   existing in this body,
     my skin freed from clothes
     caressed by the air,

I look down at
   the curve of my stomach,
    my hips and

remember your hands
   and your gentle but
       insistent fingers

now it's your turn

I've pushed you back
so you're leaning on the wall,

and when you come
you relax against it,
and I know your legs
are suddenly weak,
your body is trembling,

then as I stand,
you reach out and hold me very tightly,
you're a little confused,
you gaze around as if
you're not sure where you are,

I kiss your neck,
  look at you,
  thinking,

       now you know how I feel
       when you do it like this to me.

65

another cold light of day moment

'tell me it's not over'
I whispered it,
with the taste of you
still strong in my mouth,

'I'm not sure'
'I don't know'
and your eyes slid away from mine.

Now I know that
you always do this,
afterwards, as
we lie in a tangle of clothes,

but today
I couldn't bear it, so
I sat up,
sat away from you,

and you caressed my back,

as my tears tried to
break through my
absolute
determination
          not to cry.

I don't know what this feeling's called

no

I'm not jealous of you in a couple,

but when I'm hearing anecdotes,
or casual plans for next week,
or parties to come,
visits made and planned,

do you remember?
what time on Friday?
we
us
we

and I'm smiling,
   like a family friend does,

I wish
yes sometimes I wish that

we had
a place together

in other people's lives.

leaving

I drove away
with the taste of you
on my tongue
and your touch still
tingling on my skin

I was amazed that I could
still manage to drive as

I was suddenly
exhausted by the most
intense
desire

a little lost

I remember
    how,
when we embrace,

 you put your hands
                on me,

 spread your fingers
  and press them and
  your palms
onto my body.

I could do with that

    right now.

I think this might be it

we walked slowly and carefully
across very slippery stones
in the bright late afternoon
   down by the sea,

      and there was a
      cold cold wind,

and with the sun shimmering
on the pale water
      there seemed to be
      a few moments of
            honesty,
            closeness,
             even tenderness,

and underneath it all,
for me at least,
it seemed as if it would never feel warm again,
and there was an overwhelming sense of loss.

souvenir

you gave me a stone,
   smooth and flat
   and full of rose quartz,

I wonder if you know
it's called the love stone?

picked up on the beach,
   carried home in your pocket,
   kept to give me,

and I had always assumed
   you don't think of me
   when we're not together.

Here it is on my desk,
   showing you remembered me once,

and invested with
all my emotion.

always discreet

I want to
Lie with you
on the grass in the park,
as the sun shines.

I want to
Push you against a wall,
on a cold rainy street,
reach into your clothes and feel you already hard.

I want to
Stand before the door,
a crowded room on the other side,
lift my shirt and pull your head down to my breast.

I want you to
Kneel as the lift door closes,
and before it opens again,
kiss my stomach and bite me gently.

I want you to
begin your meeting,
and me to
start my lecture,
with our mouths still tasting of each other.

shadows

as we passed
in the dark passage

  we embraced,
   quick and hard,

only a wall away from discovery,
so so near to being found out,

but it was impossible to be that close
and not touch

Missing the Train

It's so hot in this tiny space,
  you stroke through the
    sweat on my back
as I stretch away from you
and our hips move,

  my palms,
  flat on the wall before me
    with fingers spread,
  begin to slip,

we're gasping in
almost unbearable heat
  as your hands slide round
  to my breasts,

I look to one side,
and catch sight of two wild eyed lovers
I don't really recognise,
reflected in the glass door.

Sleeping with you

I'm sitting in your bed,
Leaning on your pillows.

 When I get up,
They will regain their
     usual shape,
and the duvet will settle
      as it was before,
      ready for you,
           tonight,
      in the real world.

I'm like a ghost,
no-one can see me in your life,
         and perhaps,
when I'm not here,
   you're not entirely sure
      if I exist.

lunch out

perhaps you hoped to
shock me

sitting in the crowded cafe
talking with the others round the table

when you put your hand
up my skirt

but I think you were the more surprised
to find I was without underwear

But at the time? I thought this was right

You phoned to give an excuse,
　　But I already knew
　　you weren't coming,

And as I sat,
　　on a bench in the crowded street,
　　crying uncontrollably behind my sunglasses,

It came to me that perhaps,
　　and I could hardly bear to think it,
　　perhaps it should stop here.

I wonder if you'd miss me,
　　when I hadn't phoned for a while,
　　or arranged to see you?

I wonder if you'd finally be moved
　　to make an effort,
　　contact me, ask how I am, ask to meet,

or if in some way
　　it would be easier,
　　so very much easier and of course safer,

to have all that uncomfortable emotion
　　and wild physical passion
　　safely tucked away in your fantasy.

too late

I know you're in bed,
the bed I slept in once
when you weren't there,

in a house
   full of the shadows of us,

and I know you're drifting
into sleep.

Right now

I would give anything to imagine
and believe it,
that you were awake too,

thinking about me.

Tangled Web

I just realised
that the one person I don't lie to
is my lover,

after all

I've deceived everyone else
  to be with him,

and with him,

I don't need to disguise
 my whereabouts, or not mention
certain parts of my day, and

I'm not obliged to conceal any
 of my thoughts, or bear in mind
certain differences in bed.

In fact,

when we're together it's the one time

 I'm not exercising some restraint,
I don't have to think about what to say,
and I'm absolutely open and carefree,

But then I wonder

is he being completely open with me?

Trying

He kissed me.

I shut my eyes,
pretended,
and responded with my head full of you,
my skin growing hot.

Then he whispered my name,
and I found I could not speak.

finding a voice

   of course
it's a metaphor
     for whatever it is that
finally makes you
    serious
       about what you do,
and
          shakes you from your
  easy path
and
drags you away from
   indecision
onto a very different road,

and so
I will never do anything
other than celebrate
  that
through all of this,
through you,

come what may,

the Devil is finally interested
          in buying my soul.

the benefit of exercise

we sat by the river
feeling the sun,

and side by side
on a log by a fallen tree
shaded from the river
but next to the path

we did what all lovers do -

we talked about
    our relationship
    us
    and the world we have to inhabit,

and compelled by
 something beyond
    caution or reason

we went as far as we could go,

 stopping of course
 for passing cyclists and pedestrians

Watching my back

You have always watched as
I walk away when we part,

I'm aware of you standing still,
    Not turning.

I like it that you hold our goodbyes,

And I hate having to go.

after midnight

I put my hands in my pockets
    and
hunch my shoulders against my tears

      as you make tea
      and glance at me
      not sure what to say.

We just made love
    but
    can't sleep together

      that's how it is
      we are as we are

    but
why wouldn't I be sad?

hold on to me

confusion

heat

I remember

trying to wriggle away

but
you held me   your

hands

your
fingers

and
strength

my back arched against you

and

then

defenceless

at the moment when
there were no barriers between us,

I looked at you and realised again
how beautiful you are.

balance of power

You lift your head
turn it slightly from me
and look away

As there's never a time
when I do this to you

I've just realised
we kiss when you decide

Sssshhh

noticing you were about to cry out,
not thinking of where we were,

I reached my hand
    up to your open mouth.

  Immediately,
instinctive and abandoned,

you bit me hard
  as you came.

getting re-acquainted

we're holding a space between us
filled with intent,

standing with bodies not quite touching,

our faces very close.

you lower your head to
breathe against my neck
across my shoulders

  then your lips on my skin.

at last we kiss
quick and light

but still no words.

I think on that day it was raining

once,
you opened the front door to me
in your bathrobe

you'd just had a shower

and I
who had nearly driven by
and not stopped

thinking as always
it was over
I walked past you talking,
talking
like it was a social visit,
and afraid to look at you,

but you stopped me,
and standing before me,
made it very clear
what you wanted to do

a different perspective

it hurt

but felt good

finally

I cried out

you groaned

and then you came

I turned to you

we embraced

looked at each other

    and giggled

rain on the windscreen

but actually I need to
    feel you touch me,

when we stand together,
your arms round me, as
I rest my head against your shoulder,
and you lean down to kiss my neck.

do you know,
    I could probably count the
    number of times
    we've stood like that,
        if it weren't for these
        distracting tears.

after the seventh day

I want it

to feel your weight
on top of me

your breath
on my neck

fuck me

move
harder
faster

sweat

cry out

come

Let me tell you something

I tell you that
I love you

and you

as always

can't reply

after a while

I have real fear
after a long gap

I don't want to look at you
in case your eyes have
changed,

I don't want to talk to you
in case you are cold, formal,
polite,

or try and touch you
in case you pull away from me.

Not knowing is almost better

and being apart suddenly seems preferable

to seeing you and perhaps finding out
the absolute worst

A summer wedding in a roofless Great Hall

My feet on short damp grass

Music soaking into old brick walls
   and
  reaching through empty windows
  to the woods beyond the smooth lawns

The dancers before me in the twilight
   could have been happy ghosts
   or
    whispers of future celebrations,

all so young and so in love

Enfolded in it all as they danced
  I looked up,

Right above me was a single star,

   and I thought I could hear
   bats' wings flutter

    as I stretched to cover it with my open hand,

      Then filling my head
      with an image of you

I closed my fingers

        and made a wish.

obsession

if I'd devoted all this time to
    mastering a language
    furthering my career
       and planning my pension,

think how learned and
wealthy I would now be.

letting me in

my fears about

    how you might feel

      after all this time

disappeared

  when you opened your front door to me

entirely

naked

tea

standing by the
goodnight kettle

we kissed,
slow reflective kisses,

kisses that didn't
   anticipate immediate passion,

   or look into the future,

   or analyse,
      interpret,
      try to understand,

no,
 they were just
 kisses,
sweet slow kisses

that for a few moments
took us into our own world,

before,
as always,

we had to part.

after all the other stuff

I'd sort of forgotten
how well we get on,

as we giggled
in an increasingly hot room,
gossiped,
played with words,
egged each other on.

It was so simple, and
I was so happy that
we know each other,
that we like each other,
and
we could still be like this.

the benefits of jewellery

I'm remembering
how it looks
when I hold it,

so long and firm
     and pale

   with my tanned fingers
around it

and the bright glass beads
of my bracelet glistening,

draping down over
the back of my hand,

and shivering together
        as I move

not necessarily a whole night, but

it creates a space, whispering
no real rush,
no desperate hurry,

  we've made some time to
    explore each other,
  make love,
    then doze
      in our own happy world,
touching in the gentle way of afterwards,
relaxing,

  time to look,
   and feel emotion,
reflect,
shared breath as time folds round us.

It says
    this has meaning out of our ordinary lives,

It is a powerful thing for lovers to do.

Oh,
    of course!
that's why
  you won't do it

not at home

this evening is mocking me
with something we've never had,

ordinary time,
which just passes,
where not much happens.

I've never been able to ask you
if you want a cup of tea,

to move over
so I can put my feet up,

or watch you doze in front of the late film.

discretionary leisure

after all this time
we actually did it,

sat on the sofa
watched some TV
  and I dozed,
stretched out next to you
  with my feet resting on your leg,

earlier on we'd drunk tea and chatted,

we could have been mistaken for a couple,

or at least two very good friends

at the theatre

how can it be that
I am so desperate to feel
you touch me
that my skin is actually tingling
and sensitive to my clothes weight

I don't understand how
   my body is just sitting here
apparently relaxed
showing no sign of my desire
while my eyes watch the play
     some of the time

I want to stand up
stumble to the door
and once outside
lie on the damp grass
and howl at the
cold uncaring moon

definitely not love

it wasn't about us
or me,
no
I think
the sex was about you,
all you.

I can't remember if I was crying
  or if that was afterwards
as in the dark,
hard,
determined,
against the wall
in the room
where I work,
you fucked me.

My body responded
as it always does to you,
but I knew
it was nothing to do with the real me
and you didn't care.

You came,
we dressed at least I think we did,
and I felt hot tears on my face
as I walked,
straight backed,
up to bed.

Saturday Shopping

Today the town is full of lovers,
All in close pairs,
Exchanging public signs of private lives,

All those fingers,
lightly touching or entwined,
absolutely nothing to hide.

I put my hands deep into my pockets,
and walk on.

making breakfast

behind me
erect immediately
I reach back and guide you in

I'm wet

this is fucking
coupling like dogs

we're playing a game
marking each other

knowing
colluding
quick

you come
withdraw
giggle

turn away
and switch on the kettle

I straighten up
and start buttering the hot toast

visiting Anna

it wasn't a real mirror
but she held it up anyway

and I looked into a suddenly clear world,
where we walked arm in arm in the sunshine,
kissed on a street corner,
decided to stay in tonight,
and slept in the same bed.

it was simple,
and happy,

but it was just a mirror,

so I looked back,
back to the world I really live in.

things you say

I have no right
I have no right to say I love you
You're beautiful and should be out there
I can't offer you more than this
do you want to end it?

do you?
do you want to end it?
what do you want me to do?
no - what do you want?
I want whatever you do
I have no right to say

Isolation Road

I walked in the cruel dusk,
Light calling me from houses on either side of the street.

It seemed as if in every front room there was a family,
Happy or not they were there,
Indoors,
Contained in the glow,
Excluding the night and all that was in it.

My place is here,
I'll always be looking in,
However clearly I can see you.

I wonder if you ever raise your eyes to the cold glass,
and think about me,
Outside.

face it

here it is then

it was going
nowhere

it ended

now I'm going
nowhere

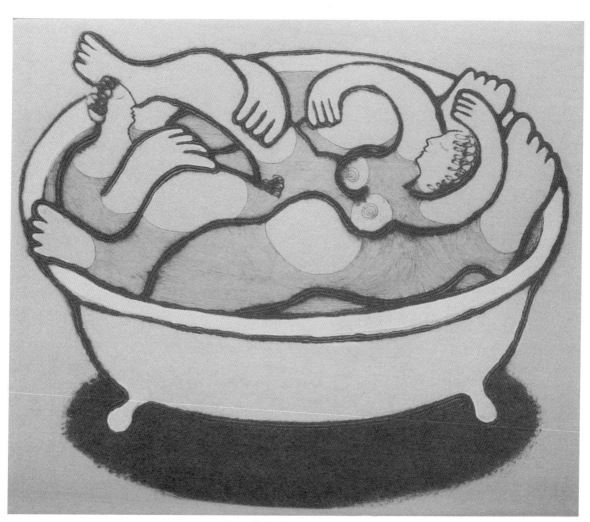

Bathing Lovers I
By Trevor Price

Trevor Price – Artist/Printmaker

Trevor Price was born in 1966 and grew up in Cornwall. He studied Printmaking at Falmouth and then Winchester School of Art. On leaving college he learned the skills of professional printmaking in a London etching studio.

In his mid-twenties Trevor returned to Cornwall basing himself in St. Ives. Influenced by the area, his work began to develop, leading him to make a living solely from his art. Trevor has since returned to London, but has maintained the St. Ives base, from where he also still works.

The Cornwall, and chiefly St. Ives, connection naturally comes through in Trevor's work. Understandably artists with a St. Ives connection, such as Ben Nicholson and William Scott, have a large influence on his work. Other artists that influence him include Picasso, Henry Moore, Elizabeth Frink and Cecil Collins.

His subject matter in some way is a reflection of his life. Some of the pieces are about the intimacy between a couple, and others show the normal obsessions of any man.

Trevor exhibits widely through Europe and regularly holds solo exhibitions of his paintings as well as original prints. His work is held in numerous collections including the Bank of England, Yale University and P&O.

His has won several national printmaking awards, and is an active member of the Royal Society of Painter-Printmakers. He has also been an invited selector for the National Printmaking Exhibition held at the Mall Galleries in London.

To view more works by Trevor Price, or to contact him directly, please visit his website at **www.trevorprice.co.uk**

MORE WELSH WRITING
FROM ACCENT PRESS LTD

The Fevered Hive
Dennis Lewis
ISBN 095486736X
A cutting edge collection of Cardiff-based, urban writing.
"High octane prose - fast and genuinely furious..."
CATHERINE MERRIMAN

Red Stilettos
Ruth Joseph
ISBN 0954489977
An intriguing and provocative collection of short stories by a Cardiff-based Jewish writer. Snapshots of family life contrast with dark tales of suffering in this multifaceted and startling collection. Ruth Joseph's unique voice reverberates with honesty and passion. She has lived trapped with these stories and memories. Now they must be heard…
"An astonishingly honest, real and utterly moving collection…"
WESTERN MAIL

An Eye of Death
George Rees
ISBN 0954709276
This rip-roaring novel illuminates life in Tudor London at the time of Shakespeare, Marlowe and Sir Walter Raleigh. Fast paced action, murder, intrigue, lust and treachery – breathtaking!
"A modern day Chaucer."
ROBERT NESBIT

TITLES AVAILABLE BY POST

To order titles from Accent Press Ltd by post, simply complete the form below and return to the address below, enclosing a cheque or postal order for the full amount plus £1 p&p per book.

	TITLE	AUTHOR	PRICE
☐	Sexy Shorts for Christmas	Various	£6.99
☐	Sexy Shorts for Lovers	Various	£6.99
☐	Sexy Shorts for Summer	Various	£6.99
☐	Scary Shorts for Halloween	Various	£6.99
☐	Why Do You Overeat?	Zoë Harcombe	£9.99
☐	The Diet Cookbook	Zoë Harcombe & Rachel McGuiness	£9.99
☐	How to Draw Cartoons	Brian Platt	£7.99
☐	Notso Fatso	Walter Whichelow	£6.99
☐	Triplet Tales	Hazel Cushion	£5.99
☐	An Eye of Death	George Rees	£7.99
☐	The Fevered Hive	Dennis Lewis	£7.99

All prices correct at time of going to press. However the publisher reserves the right to change prices without prior notice. Cheques payable to 'Accent Press Ltd'. Do not send cash. Cards not accepted.

Send this form to: PO Box 50, Pembroke Dock, Pembrokeshire, UK. SA72 6WY

NAME _____

ADDRESS _____

POSTCODE _____